CAKE & ICE CREAM

RECIPES FOR GOOD TIMES

CHRONICLE BOOKS
SAN FRANCISCO

Material on pages 6–29 previously published in *Sky High* by Alisa Huntsman and
Peter Wynne (text copyright © 2007 by King Hill Productions and photographs
copyright © 2007 by Tina Rupp) by Chronicle Books LLC.

Material on pages 30–41 previously published in *The Cupcake Deck* (text copyright
© 2007 by Elinor Klivans and photographs copyright © 2007 by France Ruffenach)
by Chronicle Books LLC.

Material on pages 42–51 previously published in *Ice Creams & Sorbets*
(text copyright © 2005 by Lou Seibert Pappas and photographs copyright © 2005
by Victoria Pearson) by Chronicle Books LLC.

Material on pages 52–63 previously published in *Ice Cream Treats*
(text copyright © 2004 by Charity Ferreira and photographs copyright © 2004
by Leigh Beisch) by Chronicle Books LLC.

Library of Congress Cataloging-in-Publication Data available.
ISBN 978-1-4521-4116-9

Manufactured in China

Design by Vanessa Dina
Illustrations by Nami Kurita

10 9 8 7 6 5 4 3 2 1

Chronicle Books LLC
680 Second Street
San Francisco, California 94107
www.chroniclebooks.com

CONTENTS

SKY-HIGH
STRAWBERRY
SHORTCAKE

19

BLACK FOREST
CAKE

23

BANANA–
CHOCOLATE
CHIP CAKE

27

BITTERSWEET
CHOCOLATE
ICE CREAM

43

CLASSIC
VANILLA BEAN
ICE CREAM

45

MINT
CHOCOLATE CHIP
ICE CREAM

47

PISTACHIO
ICE CREAM
SANDWICHES
WITH WALNUT BROWNIES

57

ICE CREAM
BONBONS

61

TRIPLE CHOCOLATE
FUDGE CAKE

WHITE CHOCOLATE MOUSSE

4 oz [110 g] white chocolate, coarsely chopped

1 cup [240 ml] heavy cream

1 egg white

1 Tbsp sugar

SOUR CREAM CHOCOLATE ICING

12 oz [340 g] bittersweet or semisweet chocolate, coarsely chopped

½ cup [115 g] unsalted butter, at room temperature

2 Tbsp light corn syrup

¼ cup [60 ml] half-and-half, at room temperature

½ cup [120 ml] sour cream, at room temperature

CAKE

2¼ cups [280 g] all-purpose flour

1 cup [100 g] unsweetened cocoa powder

2¼ tsp baking soda

1¼ tsp baking powder

1 tsp salt

½ tsp ground cinnamon

2½ oz [70 g] unsweetened chocolate, coarsely chopped

1 cup [240 ml] milk

1¼ cups [300 ml] hot, strongly brewed coffee

2 eggs

1 cup [225 g] mayonnaise

1½ tsp vanilla extract

2¼ cups [450 g] sugar

CONT'D

TO MAKE THE WHITE CHOCOLATE MOUSSE: Melt the white chocolate with ¼ cup [60 ml] of the cream in a double boiler or a small heatproof bowl set over a pan of very hot water. Whisk until smooth. Remove from the heat and let the white chocolate cream cool to room temperature.

In a large bowl, beat the remaining ¾ cup [180 ml] heavy cream until soft peaks form. In a clean bowl, whip the egg white with the sugar until fairly stiff peaks form.

Fold the beaten egg white into the white chocolate cream, then fold in the whipped cream just until blended. Err on the side of undermixing. Cover the mousse and refrigerate while you make the icing and the cake.

TO MAKE THE SOUR CREAM CHOCOLATE ICING: Melt the chocolate with the butter and corn syrup in a double boiler or a small heatproof bowl set over a pan of barely simmering water. Remove from the heat and whisk until smooth.

Whisk in the half-and-half and sour cream. Cover the bowl and set aside at room temperature while you make the cake.

TO MAKE THE CAKE: Preheat the oven to 350°F [180°C]. Butter the bottoms and sides of three 9-in [23-cm] round cake pans. Line the bottom of each pan with a round of parchment paper and butter the paper.

Sift together the flour, cocoa powder, baking soda, baking powder, salt, and cinnamon. Set the dry ingredients aside.

Put the chocolate in a fairly large heatproof bowl. In a small saucepan, bring the milk to a simmer. Pour the hot coffee and milk over the chocolate. Let stand for a minute, then whisk until smooth. Let the mocha liquid cool slightly.

In the bowl of an electric mixer, beat together the eggs, mayonnaise, and vanilla until well blended. Gradually beat in the sugar. Add the dry ingredients and mocha liquid alternately in two or three additions, beating until smooth and well blended after each addition. Divide the batter among the three prepared cake pans.

Bake for 25 to 28 minutes, or until a cake tester or wooden toothpick inserted in the center comes out almost clean. Let the cakes cool in their pans on wire racks for 10 to 15 minutes. Unmold onto the racks; carefully peel off the papers and let cool completely, at least 1 hour. (The layers can be baked a day ahead; wrap well and refrigerate.)

Place a cake layer, flat-side up, on a cake stand or serving plate. Cover the top evenly with half the mousse, leaving a ¼-in [6-mm] margin around the edge. Repeat with the second layer and the remaining mousse. Set the third layer on top and pour half the icing over the filled cake. Spread all over the sides and top. Don't worry if some of the cake shows through. This first frosting is to seal in the crumbs, which is why professionals call it a "crumb coat." Refrigerate, uncovered, for at least 30 minutes to allow the icing to set. Cover the rest of the icing and set aside at room temperature.

Frost the top and sides of the cake with the remaining icing, which should have the consistency of mayonnaise. If the icing has become too soft, chill briefly; if it is too stiff, microwave on high for just 2 or 3 seconds to soften, then stir to mix well. Use an offset palette knife or the back of a spoon to swirl the frosting decoratively around the cake. Slice and serve.

MAKES ONE 9-IN [23-CM] TRIPLE-LAYER CAKE

SOUTHERN COCONUT CAKE

CREAM CHEESE
BUTTERCREAM FROSTING

12 oz [340 g] cream cheese,
slightly chilled

¾ cup plus 2 Tbsp [195 g]
unsalted butter, at room
temperature

1 cup [120 g] powdered sugar,
sifted after measuring

2 tsp vanilla extract

1 cup [200 g] granulated sugar

¼ cup [60 ml] water

3 egg whites

CAKE

5 egg whites

½ cup [120 ml] milk

2 tsp vanilla extract

3 cups [250 g] cake flour

2⅓ cups [475 g] granulated sugar

4½ tsp baking powder

½ tsp salt

1 cup [225 g] unsalted butter,
at warm room temperature

1 cup [240 g] unsweetened
coconut milk

2½ cups [200 g] sweetened
flaked coconut

TO MAKE THE CREAM CHEESE BUTTERCREAM FROSTING: Place the
cream cheese in the bowl of a mixer and beat on medium speed
until slightly fluffy and smooth. Add the butter 2 Tbsp at a time,

CONT'D

11

mixing until smooth. Add the powdered sugar and vanilla and mix until fluffy. Set aside at room temperature.

Combine the granulated sugar and water in a small heavy saucepan and bring to a boil over medium heat, stirring to dissolve the sugar. Continue to cook, without stirring, until the syrup reaches the soft-ball stage, 240°F [115°C] on a candy thermometer.

Meanwhile, put the egg whites in the bowl of an electric mixer fitted with the whisk attachment. When the syrup is ready, turn the mixer to medium-low speed and begin beating the egg whites. Slowly add the hot syrup to the whites, taking care not to pour it directly onto the beater, or it may splash out of the bowl and burn you. When all of the syrup is incorporated, raise the speed to medium-high and beat until the egg white mixture has cooled to body temperature and a stiff meringue forms.

With the mixer on low speed, begin adding the cream cheese mixture by the spoonful. When all of the cream cheese mixture has been incorporated, raise the speed to medium and whip until the frosting is smooth and fluffy. Cover the bowl and refrigerate while you make the cake.

TO MAKE THE CAKE: Preheat the oven to 350°F [180°C]. Butter the bottoms of three 8-in [20-cm] round cake pans or coat with cooking spray. Line the bottom of each pan with a round of parchment and butter the paper.

Put the egg whites in a mixing bowl and whisk slightly. Add the milk and vanilla and whisk to mix thoroughly; set aside.

In another bowl, combine the flour, granulated sugar, baking powder, and salt. Beat on low speed to mix well and break up any lumps, about 30 seconds. Add the butter and coconut milk and, with the mixer still on low, beat to combine. Raise the speed to medium and beat until light and fluffy, about 2 minutes.

Add the egg white mixture in two or three additions, scraping down the sides of the bowl and mixing just long enough to incorporate between additions. Divide the batter among the three prepared pans.

Bake for 30 minutes, or until a cake tester or wooden toothpick inserted in the center comes out clean. Let the cakes cool in their pans for 10 minutes. Then turn them out onto cooling racks and allow to cool completely.

Place a cake layer, flat-side up, on an 8-in [20-cm] cardboard cake round. Cover this layer with 1 cup [400 g] of the buttercream frosting, spreading it evenly right to the edge. Sprinkle ½ cup [40 g] of the coconut over the frosting. Add the second layer of cake and repeat with another 1 cup [400 g] frosting and ½ cup [40 g] coconut. Top with the final layer of cake and frost the top and sides with the remaining frosting.

Place the remaining 1½ cups [120 g] coconut on a large baking tray. Pick up the cake and hold it on the palm of one hand over the tray. Using the other hand, scoop up some of the coconut and press it onto the side of the cake. Continue to do this, rotating the cake slightly each time, until the sides are completely coated. Set the cake on a serving plate and sprinkle any remaining coconut over the top. Chill for at least 1 hour to allow the frosting to firm up before slicing.

MAKES ONE 8-IN [20-CM] TRIPLE-LAYER CAKE

SOUR CREAM–CHOCOLATE CAKE

WITH PEANUT BUTTER FROSTING AND CHOCOLATE–PEANUT BUTTER GLAZE

CAKE

2 cups [255 g] all-purpose flour

2½ cups [500 g] granulated sugar

¾ cup [60 g] unsweetened,
Dutch-process cocoa powder

2 tsp baking soda

1 tsp salt

1 cup [240 ml] neutral vegetable
oil, such as canola, soybean, or
vegetable blend

1 cup [240 ml] sour cream

1½ cups [360 ml] water

2 Tbsp distilled white vinegar

1 tsp vanilla extract

2 eggs

PEANUT BUTTER FROSTING

10 oz [280 g] cream cheese,
at room temperature

½ cup [115 g] unsalted butter,
at room temperature

5 cups [500 g] powdered sugar,
sifted

⅔ cup [175 g] smooth peanut
butter

CHOCOLATE–PEANUT BUTTER GLAZE

8 oz [220 g] semisweet chocolate,
coarsely chopped

3 Tbsp smooth peanut butter

2 Tbsp light corn syrup

½ cup [120 ml] half-and-half

CONT'D

TO MAKE THE CAKE: Preheat the oven to 350°F [180°C]. Butter the bottoms and sides of three 8-in [20-cm] round cake pans. Line the bottom of each pan with a round of parchment and butter the paper.

Sift the flour, granulated sugar, cocoa powder, baking soda, and salt into a large bowl. Whisk to combine them well. Add the oil and sour cream and whisk to blend. Gradually beat in the water. Blend in the vinegar and vanilla. Whisk in the eggs and beat until well blended. Scrape down the sides of the bowl and be sure the batter is well mixed. Divide among the three prepared cake pans.

Bake for 30 to 35 minutes, or until a cake tester or wooden toothpick inserted in the center comes out almost clean. Let cool in the pans for about 20 minutes, then invert onto wire racks, carefully peel off the paper, and let cool completely. While the cake layers are cooling, make the frosting and glaze.

TO MAKE THE PEANUT BUTTER FROSTING: In the bowl of an electric mixer, beat the cream cheese and butter until light and fluffy. Gradually add the powdered sugar 1 cup [100 g] at a time, mixing thoroughly after each addition and scraping down the sides of the bowl often. Continue to beat on medium speed until light and fluffy, 3 to 4 minutes.

Add the peanut butter and beat until thoroughly blended. Set aside while you make the glaze.

TO MAKE THE CHOCOLATE–PEANUT BUTTER GLAZE: In the top of
a double boiler or in a heatproof bowl set over simmering water,
combine the chocolate, peanut butter, and corn syrup. Whisk until
the chocolate is melted and the mixture is smooth.

Remove from the heat and whisk in the half-and-half, beating
until smooth. Use while still warm.

Place a cake layer, flat-side up, on a cake stand or large serving
plate. Spread ⅔ cup [130 g] of the frosting evenly over the top.
Repeat with the next layer. Place the last layer on top and frost
the top and sides of the cake with the remaining frosting.

To decorate with the glaze, put the cake plate on a large baking
sheet to catch any drips. Simply pour the glaze over the top of the
cake and, using an offset spatula, spread it evenly over the top just
to the edges so that it runs down the sides of the cake in long drips.
Refrigerate, uncovered, for at least 30 minutes to allow the glaze
and frosting to set completely. Remove from the refrigerator about
1 hour before serving.

MAKES ONE 8-IN [20-CM] TRIPLE-LAYER CAKE

SKY-HIGH
STRAWBERRY SHORTCAKE

FRESH STRAWBERRY FILLING

2 pt [910 g] small strawberries

2 tsp rose water or 2 Tbsp anisette liqueur

2 tsp vanilla extract

½ cup [100 g] sugar

CAKE

5 Tbsp [70 g] unsalted butter, at room temperature

¾ cup [170 g] sugar

1 tsp vanilla extract

2 eggs

1½ cups [185 g] cake flour

2½ tsp baking powder

Pinch of salt

⅔ cup [165 ml] buttermilk

1½ cups [360 ml] heavy cream

2 Tbsp sugar

Whole strawberries for garnish

TO MAKE THE FRESH STRAWBERRY FILLING: Clean and hull the berries and slice into pieces about the thickness of a coin. Place in a bowl and add the rose water, vanilla, and sugar. Stir to coat, cover the bowl, and let the berries macerate at room temperature until they exude their juices, about 1 hour.

CONT'D

TO MAKE THE CAKE: Preheat the oven to 350°F [180°C]. Butter the bottoms and sides of three 6-in [15-cm] round cake pans. Line the bottom of each with a round of parchment and butter the paper.

In the bowl of an electric mixer, cream the butter, ¾ cup [170 g] sugar, and vanilla until light and fluffy. Add the eggs one at a time, scraping down the sides of the bowl well after each addition.

Sift together the flour, baking powder, and salt. Add these dry ingredients to the batter, alternating with the buttermilk in two or three additions. Divide the batter among the three prepared cake pans.

Bake for 20 to 25 minutes, or until a cake tester or wooden toothpick inserted in the center comes out clean. Let cool in the pans for 10 minutes; then invert onto wire racks, carefully peel off the paper, and allow to cool completely.

In a large chilled mixing bowl with chilled beaters, whip the cream with the remaining 2 Tbsp sugar until stiff. There will be about 3 cups [300 g] when whipped.

Place a cake layer, flat-side up, on a small cake stand or a serving plate. Top with ¾ cup [130 g] of the strawberry filling, spooning it over the entire layer and making sure any juices go onto the cake layer and not the plate, if possible. Top this with 1 cup [100 g] of the whipped cream, spreading it evenly over the berries. Repeat with the second cake layer and another ¾ cup [130 g] filling and 1 cup [100 g] whipped cream. Top the final cake layer flat-side up. Garnish with a few whole berries and top with the last of the whipped cream. For the best flavor, cover the dessert with a cake dome or loose plastic wrap and refrigerate for about 2 hours before slicing. Serve with the remaining strawberry filling on the side.

MAKES ONE 6-IN [15-CM] TRIPLE-LAYER CAKE

BLACK FOREST CAKE

BRANDIED CHERRIES

1 lb [455 g] dark, sweet cherries, pitted

½ cup [120 ml] kirsch

CAKE

¾ cup plus 2 Tbsp [105 g] cake flour

¾ cup [60 g] unsweetened cocoa powder

7 eggs

1½ cups [200 g] sugar

3 cups [720 ml] heavy cream

¼ cup [50 g] sugar

1½ tsp vanilla extract

Chilled chocolate curls for decoration

TO MAKE THE BRANDIED CHERRIES: Put the cherries and kirsch into a glass container with a lid. Refrigerate for several hours, or up to several days. For use, drain the cherries well, reserving the liquor in which they steeped.

TO MAKE THE CAKE: Preheat the oven to 350°F [180°C]. Line the bottoms of three 9-in [23-cm] round cake pans with rounds of parchment paper but do not grease the pans.

CONT'D

Sift together the cake flour and cocoa powder. Set this mixture aside.

In the bowl of an electric mixer, beat the eggs to blend. Gradually add the 1½ cups [200 g] sugar and beat on medium-high speed until a slowly dissolving ribbon forms when the beaters are lifted.

Sift one-third of the dry ingredients over the egg mixture. With a rubber spatula, gently fold in. Repeat this step twice more, then fold the batter until the ingredients are well mixed, without deflating the batter. Divide the batter among the three prepared pans.

Bake for about 20 minutes, or until a cake tester or wooden toothpick inserted into the center comes out clean. Remove from the oven and let the layers cool in their pans completely, at least 1 hour. To unmold, run a blunt knife around the edges of the pan and invert; peel off the paper.

In a large, chilled mixing bowl with chilled beaters, beat the cream until it mounds lightly. Add the remaining ¼ cup [50 g] sugar and the vanilla and whip until the cream is fairly stiff.

Place a cake layer, flat-side up, on a cake stand or serving plate and sprinkle 2 to 3 Tbsp of the reserved cherry brandy evenly over the top to moisten. Cover the cake with ⅔ cup [65 g] of the whipped cream, spreading it all the way up to the edge. Set aside a small handful of cherries and then arrange half of the remaining cherries on top of the whipped cream. Cover the cherries with another ⅔ cup [65 g] of the whipped cream. Repeat with the second layer. Put the third cake layer on top and moisten it with the remaining cherry brandy. Frost the entire cake—top and sides—with whipped cream.

To decorate, gently scoop up the chilled chocolate curls with your hands and press them onto the sides of the cake, covering it completely with the curls. Decorate the top with rosettes of whipped cream and the reserved cherries. Refrigerate the cake for several hours before serving. This will make it much easier to cut and serve.

MAKES ONE 9-IN [23-CM] TRIPLE-LAYER CAKE

BANANA–CHOCOLATE CHIP CAKE

CAKE

2¼ cups [285 g] cake flour

1⅓ cups [265 g] sugar

1¼ tsp baking powder

1¼ tsp baking soda

1 tsp ground cinnamon

1 tsp Chinese five-spice powder

½ tsp salt

½ cup plus 1 Tbsp [130 g] unsalted butter, at room temperature

1 cup [280 g] mashed very ripe bananas

3 eggs

¾ cup [180 ml] buttermilk

1½ tsp vanilla extract

¾ cup [170 g] mini semisweet chocolate chips

CARAMEL DRIZZLE

1 cup [240 ml] prepared thick caramel sauce, such as cajeta

3 Tbsp dark rum

1½ cups [360 ml] heavy cream

3 Tbsp sugar

2 ripe but firm bananas, thinly sliced

Mini semisweet chocolate chips for decoration

TO MAKE THE CAKE: Preheat the oven to 350°F [180°C]. Butter the bottoms of three 8-in [20-cm] round cake pans or coat with cooking spray. Line the bottom of each pan with a round of parchment paper and butter the paper.

CONT'D

Place the flour, sugar, baking powder, baking soda, cinnamon, five-spice powder, and salt in a large bowl. Beat on low speed, blending well, about 1 minute. Add the butter and mashed bananas and beat until well blended. Raise the speed to medium and beat until light and fluffy, about 3 minutes.

Combine the eggs, buttermilk, and vanilla in a small bowl and whisk to blend. Add to the batter in three additions, scraping the bowl well and beating just until blended after each addition. Finally, fold in half of the chocolate chips by hand. Divide the batter among the three prepared cake pans. Sprinkle the remaining chocolate chips on top.

Bake for 25 to 28 minutes, or until a cake tester or wooden toothpick inserted in the center comes out clean. Let cool in the pans for 10 to 15 minutes, then invert onto wire racks. Carefully peel off the paper and let cool completely.

TO MAKE THE CARAMEL DRIZZLE: Put the caramel sauce in a small heavy saucepan and warm over low heat, stirring, just until heated through, about 2 minutes. Remove from the heat and whisk in the rum. Let cool to room temperature before using.

In a large, chilled mixing bowl with chilled beaters, whip the cream with the remaining 3 Tbsp sugar until stiff.

Place a cake layer, flat-side up, on a cake stand or serving plate. Top with 2 to 3 Tbsp of the caramel drizzle and spread it thinly but evenly over the whole layer. Arrange about half the banana slices on top in a single layer. Cover the bananas with 1 cup [100 g] of the whipped cream, spreading it evenly over the layer. Repeat with the second layer, adding more caramel, bananas, and cream. Place the final cake layer on top and coat it with 2 to 3 Tbsp of caramel; reserve the remaining caramel to serve with the cake slices. Dollop on the remaining whipped cream, a few more banana slices, and sprinkle the top with chocolate chips, if you like.

MAKES ONE 8-IN [20-CM] TRIPLE-LAYER CAKE

CHOCOLATE CUPCAKES
WITH CHOCOLATE BUTTERCREAM FROSTING

CUPCAKES

3 oz [85 g] unsweetened chocolate, finely chopped

1 cup [125 g] unbleached all-purpose flour

½ tsp baking powder

½ tsp baking soda

¼ tsp salt

½ cup [225 g] unsalted butter, at room temperature

1¼ cups [250 g] granulated sugar

2 eggs

1 tsp vanilla extract

½ cup [120 ml] sour cream

½ cup [120 ml] water

FROSTING

3 oz [85 g] unsweetened chocolate, chopped

2½ cups [250 g] powdered sugar

1½ Tbsp unsweetened Dutch-process cocoa powder

1½ cups [340 g] unsalted butter, at room temperature

1 tsp vanilla extract

½ cup [120 ml] heavy cream, at room temperature

4 oz [110 g] dark chocolate shavings

TO MAKE THE CUPCAKES: Position a rack in the middle of the oven. Preheat the oven to 350°F [180°C]. Line 18 muffin tin cups with paper cupcake liners.

CONT'D

Melt the chocolate in a double boiler or in a small heatproof bowl set over a pan of simmering water. Stir until the chocolate is melted and smooth. Remove from the heat and set aside to cool slightly.

Sift the flour, baking powder, baking soda, and salt into a medium bowl and set aside.

In the bowl of an electric mixer, beat the butter and granulated sugar on medium speed until smoothly blended and creamy, about 2 minutes. Stop the mixer and scrape the sides of the bowl as needed during mixing. On low speed, mix in the melted chocolate. On medium speed, add the eggs one at a time, mixing until each is blended into the batter. Add the vanilla and beat until the mixture looks creamy, about 1 minute. Mix in the sour cream until no white streaks remain. On low speed, add half of the flour mixture, mixing just to incorporate it. Mix in the water, then the remaining flour mixture, until it is incorporated and the batter looks smooth. Fill each paper liner to about ½ in [12 mm] below the top of the liner.

Bake just until the top feels firm and a toothpick inserted in the center comes out clean, about 20 minutes. Cool the cupcakes for 10 minutes in the pans on wire racks. Transfer the cupcakes from the pan onto a wire rack and let cool completely.

TO MAKE THE FROSTING: Melt the chocolate in a double boiler or in a small heatproof bowl set over a pan of simmering water. Stir until the chocolate is melted and smooth. Remove from the heat and set aside to cool slightly.

Sift the powdered sugar and cocoa powder into a clean bowl for the electric mixer. Add the butter and mix on low speed until smoothly blended, about 2 minutes. At first, the mixture will look crumbly but then it will form a smooth mass. Beat in the melted chocolate. Add the vanilla and cream, mixing to incorporate. On medium speed, beat the frosting for at least 3 minutes, until it looks smooth and creamy and the color lightens.

Use a small spatula to spread about 3 Tbsp of frosting on top of each cupcake, mounding the frosting in the center. Sprinkle the chocolate shavings over the tops of the cupcakes before serving.

MAKES 18 CUPCAKES

KID-SIMPLE CUPCAKES

CUPCAKES

1¼ cups [155 g] unbleached all-purpose flour

½ tsp baking powder

½ tsp baking soda

Pinch of salt

1 egg, plus 1 egg yolk

1 cup [200 g] granulated sugar

½ cup [100 g] canola or corn oil

1 tsp vanilla extract

½ cup [120 ml] sour cream

FROSTING

½ cup [115 g] unsalted butter, at room temperature

3 cups [300 g] powdered sugar

1 tsp vanilla extract

3 to 4 Tbsp milk

3 Tbsp colored sugar, nonpareils, sprinkles, candies, or finely chopped chocolate (optional)

TO MAKE THE CUPCAKES: Position a rack in the middle of the oven. Preheat the oven to 350°F [180°C]. Line 12 muffin tin cups with paper cupcake liners.

CONT'D

35

Sift the flour, baking powder, baking soda, and salt into a medium bowl and set aside.

In the bowl of an electric mixer, beat the egg, egg yolk, and granulated sugar on medium speed until thickened and lightened, about 2 minutes. Stop the mixer and scrape the sides of the bowl as needed. On low speed, mix in the oil and vanilla. Mix in the sour cream until no white streaks remain. Mix in the flour mixture until the batter is smooth. Fill each paper liner to about ½ in [12 mm] below the top of the liner.

Bake just until the top feels firm and a toothpick inserted in the center comes out clean, about 23 minutes. Cool the cupcakes for 10 minutes in the pan on a wire rack. Transfer the cupcakes from the pan onto a wire rack and let cool completely.

TO MAKE THE FROSTING: In a clean bowl for the electric mixer, beat the butter, powdered sugar, vanilla, and 3 Tbsp of the milk on low speed. Add up to 1 Tbsp more milk if needed to form a creamy, spreadable frosting.

Use a small spatula to spread a generous spoonful of frosting over the top of each cupcake. Sprinkle the frosting lightly with colored sugar, nonpareils, sprinkles, candies, or finely chopped chocolate, if desired, holding each cupcake upside down and dipping just the frosted center or edges in the decorations to make a nice pattern before serving.

MAKES 12 CUPCAKES

SPIDERWEB PUMPKIN GINGER CUPCAKES

CUPCAKES

1½ cups [185 g] unbleached all-purpose flour

¾ tsp baking powder

¾ tsp baking soda

Pinch of salt

1 tsp ground cinnamon

1 tsp ground ginger

½ cup [115 g] unsalted butter, melted and cooled slightly

1 cup [200 g] granulated sugar

1 cup [250 g] canned pumpkin (not pumpkin pie filling)

3 eggs

¼ cup [45 g] crystallized ginger cut into ⅛- to ¼-in [4- to 6-mm] pieces

FROSTING

½ cup [115 g] unsalted butter, at room temperature

6 oz [170 g] cream cheese, at room temperature

1 tsp vanilla extract

3 cups [300 g] powdered sugar

½ to 1 tsp ground cinnamon

1 to 2 tsp milk

TO MAKE THE CUPCAKES: Position a rack in the middle of the oven. Preheat the oven to 325°F [165°C]. Line 12 muffin tin cups with paper cupcake liners.

CONT'D

Sift the flour, baking powder, baking soda, salt, cinnamon, and ginger into a medium bowl and set aside. In the bowl of an electric mixer, beat the melted butter, granulated sugar, and pumpkin on low-medium speed until smoothly blended. Mix in the eggs and crystallized ginger. On low speed, mix in the flour mixture until it is incorporated. The batter will be thick. Fill each paper liner to about ½ in [12 mm] below the top of the liner.

Bake just until the top feels firm and a toothpick inserted in the center comes out clean, about 25 minutes. Cool the cupcakes for 10 minutes in the pan on a wire rack. Transfer the cupcakes from the pan onto a wire rack and let cool completely.

TO MAKE THE FROSTING: In the bowl of an electric mixer, beat the butter, cream cheese, and vanilla on low speed until smooth and thoroughly blended, about 1 minute. Stop the mixer and scrape down the sides of the bowl as needed during mixing. Add the powdered sugar, mixing until smooth, about 1 minute, then beat on medium speed for 1 minute to lighten the frosting further.

Transfer ¼ cup [60 g] of the frosting to a small bowl and stir in enough of the cinnamon to turn it a light brown color and enough of the milk to make a thick but pourable frosting. Set aside to use for the spiderweb decoration.

Use a small spatula to spread a scant ¼ cup [60 g] of the remaining frosting on top of each cupcake in a smooth, even layer.

Spoon the reserved cinnamon frosting into a small self-sealing freezer bag. Press out the excess air and seal the bag. Cut a tiny hole in one corner of the bag. Hold the bag about ½ in [12 mm] above a cupcake and slowly pipe two circles, one inside the other, on the frosting. Pipe a dot of the frosting in the center. Beginning at the center, draw the tip of a toothpick gently through the frosting toward the edge of the cupcake. Move the toothpick to the left about ¾ in [2 cm] and, beginning at the edge of the cupcake, draw it toward the center. Continue tracing lines from center to rim and rim to center, alternating the direction of the toothpick, around the top of the cupcake to form a web pattern. Repeat with the remaining cupcakes before serving.

MAKES 12 CUPCAKES

BITTERSWEET CHOCOLATE ICE CREAM

2 cups [480 ml] half-and-half or whole milk

3 egg yolks

⅔ cup [130 g] sugar

6 oz [165 g] bittersweet chocolate, chopped

1 oz [28 g] unsweetened chocolate, chopped

1 cup [240 ml] heavy cream

1 tsp vanilla extract

Prepare a large bowl or pan of ice water, to be used as an ice bath.

In the top of a double boiler or in a heatproof bowl, heat the half-and-half over simmering water until steaming. Whisk the egg yolks in a bowl until blended, then whisk in the sugar. Whisk in some hot half-and-half and then pour the yolk mixture back into the top of the double boiler. Stir and cook over the simmering water until the mixture forms a custard and coats the back of the spoon, about 10 minutes. Stir in the bittersweet and unsweetened chocolates and continue to stir until the chocolate is melted.

Immediately set the custard-filled pan in the ice bath and stir the custard occasionally until it cools to room temperature. Transfer to a container and stir in the cream and vanilla. Cover and refrigerate until thoroughly chilled.

Freeze the chilled custard mixture in an ice-cream maker according to the manufacturer's instructions. Transfer to a container, cover, and freeze until firm, about 2 hours before serving.

MAKES ABOUT 1 QT [960 ML]

CLASSIC VANILLA BEAN ICE CREAM

One 4-in [10-cm] vanilla bean

2 cups [480 ml] half-and-half or whole milk

4 egg yolks

⅔ cup [130 g] sugar

1 cup [240 ml] heavy cream

Prepare a large bowl or pan of ice water, to be used as an ice bath.

Split the vanilla bean in half lengthwise and scrape the black seeds into the top of a double boiler or a heatproof bowl. Add the pod and the half-and-half, and heat over simmering water until steaming. Whisk the egg yolks in a bowl until blended, then whisk in the sugar. Whisk in some of the hot half-and-half and then pour the yolk mixture back into the top of the double boiler. Stir and cook over the simmering water until the mixture forms a custard and coats the back of the spoon, about 10 minutes.

Immediately set the custard-filled pan in the ice bath and stir the custard occasionally until it cools to room temperature. Transfer to a container and stir in the cream. Cover and refrigerate until thoroughly chilled. Remove the vanilla pod with a fork.

Freeze the chilled custard in an ice-cream maker according to the manufacturer's instructions. Transfer to a container, cover, and freeze until firm, about 2 hours before serving.

MAKES ABOUT 1 QT [960 ML]

MINT CHOCOLATE CHIP ICE CREAM

2 cups [480 ml] half-and-half or whole milk

4 egg yolks

½ cup [100 g] sugar

1 cup [240 ml] heavy cream

2 tsp peppermint extract

3 oz [85 g] bittersweet chocolate, finely shaved

Prepare a large bowl or pan of ice water, to be used as an ice bath.

In the top of a double boiler or in a heatproof bowl, heat the half-and-half over simmering water until steaming. Whisk the egg yolks in a bowl until blended, then whisk in the sugar. Whisk in some of the hot half-and-half and then pour the yolk mixture back into the top of the double boiler. Stir and cook over the simmering water until the mixture forms a custard and coats the back of the spoon, about 10 minutes.

Immediately set the custard-filled pan in the ice bath and stir the custard occasionally until it cools to room temperature. Transfer to a container and stir in the cream and peppermint extract. Cover and refrigerate until thoroughly chilled.

Freeze the chilled custard in an ice-cream maker according to the manufacturer's instructions. When the ice cream is almost frozen, add the chocolate and churn until blended in, about 15 seconds. Transfer to a container, cover, and freeze until firm, about 2 hours before serving.

MAKES ABOUT 1 QT [960 ML]

STRAWBERRY ICE CREAM

1 cup [240 ml] heavy cream

½ cup [120 ml] half-and-half or whole milk

3 egg yolks

¾ cup [150 g] sugar

2½ cups [570 g] fresh strawberries, hulled

1 Tbsp freshly squeezed lemon juice

Prepare a large bowl or pan of ice water, to be used as an ice bath.

In the top of a double boiler or in a heatproof bowl, heat the cream and half-and-half over simmering water until steaming. Whisk the egg yolks in a bowl until blended, then whisk in ½ cup [100 g] of the sugar. Whisk in some of the hot cream and then pour the yolk mixture back into the top of the double boiler. Stir and cook over the simmering water until the mixture forms a custard and coats the back of the spoon, about 10 minutes.

Immediately set the custard-filled pan in the ice bath and stir the custard occasionally until it cools to room temperature.

While the custard cools, mash the strawberries with a potato masher, sprinkle with the remaining ¼ cup [50 g] sugar and the lemon juice, and let stand until the sugar dissolves. Stir into the custard and transfer to a container. Cover and refrigerate until thoroughly chilled.

Freeze the chilled custard in an ice-cream maker according to the manufacturer's instructions. Transfer to a container, cover, and freeze until firm, about 2 hours before serving.

MAKES ABOUT 1 QT [960 ML]

BLUEBERRY ICE CREAM

2 cups [340 g] fresh blueberries

2 Tbsp water

2 tsp grated lemon zest, plus 1 Tbsp freshly squeezed lemon juice

⅔ cup [130 g] sugar

1½ cups [360 ml] half-and-half or whole milk

1 cup [240 ml] heavy cream

1 tsp vanilla extract

2 Tbsp honey liqueur or framboise (optional)

Rinse the berries and pick out any bad ones. Place the berries in a saucepan with the water and cook over low heat until tender, about 10 minutes. Let cool slightly and purée in a blender or food processor.

Mash the lemon zest with 1 tsp of the sugar to release the oils.

In a microwave or a saucepan, heat the half-and-half with the remaining sugar, stirring until dissolved; let cool to room temperature. Stir in the blueberry purée, cream, sugared zest, lemon juice, and vanilla. Transfer to a container, cover, and refrigerate until thoroughly chilled.

Freeze the chilled berry mixture in an ice-cream maker according to the manufacturer's instructions. When the ice cream is almost frozen, spoon in the liqueur and churn until blended, about 1 minute. Transfer to a container, cover, and freeze until firm, about 2 hours before serving.

MAKES ABOUT 1 QT [960 ML]

COFFEE-TOFFEE
ICE CREAM SANDWICHES

WITH OATMEAL COOKIES

OATMEAL COOKIES

½ cup [115 g] unsalted butter, at room temperature

1 cup [220 g] packed dark brown sugar

1 egg

½ tsp vanilla extract

¾ cup plus 2 Tbsp [105 g] all-purpose flour

¾ cup [60 g] old-fashioned rolled oats

½ tsp baking soda

Pinch of salt

½ cup [60 g] toasted almonds, chopped

CHOCOLATE GLAZE

8 oz [225 g] bittersweet chocolate, finely chopped

2 Tbsp unsalted butter

2 pt [960 ml] premium coffee-toffee ice cream

TO MAKE THE OATMEAL COOKIES: In the bowl of an electric mixer fitted with the paddle attachment, beat the butter and brown sugar together on medium-high speed until well blended. Beat in the egg and vanilla, scraping down the sides of the bowl as necessary. In a small bowl, stir together the flour, oats, baking soda, and salt; beat the flour mixture into the butter mixture. Stir in the almonds. Cover and refrigerate the dough until thoroughly chilled, at least 8 hours or overnight.

CONT'D

Preheat the oven to 350°F [180°C]. With lightly floured hands, roll the dough into ¾-in [2-cm] balls and place them 2 to 3 in [5.5 to 7 cm] apart on parchment paper–lined baking sheets. Bake until the cookies are spread out and well browned, 12 to 15 minutes. Cool completely before removing from the baking sheets.

TO MAKE THE CHOCOLATE GLAZE: Bring about 2 in [5 cm] water to a boil in a saucepan or the bottom of a double boiler; remove from the heat. Combine the chocolate and butter in a heatproof bowl or in the top of the double boiler. Set the bowl over the hot water and let stand, stirring occasionally with a flexible spatula, until melted and smooth, about 15 minutes.

To assemble, place the cookies in a single layer on plates or baking sheets. Using a pastry brush or knife, brush or spread the chocolate glaze on the tops of the cookies. Chill until set, about 15 minutes, or let stand at room temperature until the glaze is completely set, about 1½ hours.

Soften the ice cream slightly. Place a large scoop of ice cream on the flat (bottom) side of one cookie; top with another cookie, bottom-side down. Press gently to compress the ice cream and bring it out to the edges of the cookies. Repeat the process to fill the remaining cookies with ice cream. Serve the sandwiches immediately, or wrap them individually in plastic wrap and freeze for up to 1 week.

MAKES ABOUT 12 SANDWICHES

PISTACHIO ICE CREAM SANDWICHES

WITH WALNUT BROWNIES

WALNUT BROWNIES

6 Tbsp [85 g] unsalted butter, cut in ½-in [12-mm] pieces

5 oz [140 g] unsweetened chocolate, chopped

1½ cups [300 g] sugar

5 eggs

1 tsp vanilla extract

¾ cup [90 g] all-purpose flour

½ tsp baking powder

Pinch of salt

1 cup [130 g] walnut pieces

2 pt [960 ml] premium pistachio ice cream

TO MAKE THE WALNUT BROWNIES: Butter a 10½-by-15-in [26.5-by-30-cm] jelly-roll pan. Line the bottom of the pan with parchment paper and butter the parchment. Lightly dust the pan with flour.

Preheat the oven to 350°F [180°C]. Bring about 2 in [5 cm] of water to a boil in a saucepan or the bottom of a double boiler; remove from the heat. Combine the butter and chocolate in a heatproof bowl or in the top of the double boiler. Set the bowl over the hot water and let stand, stirring occasionally with a flexible spatula, until melted and smooth, about 15 minutes.

CONT'D

In another bowl, whisk together the sugar, eggs, and vanilla just to blend. Stir the melted chocolate into the egg mixture until incorporated. In another bowl, stir together the flour, baking powder, and salt. Stir the flour mixture into the chocolate mixture until blended.

Spread the batter evenly in the prepared pan and sprinkle the walnuts over the top. Bake until the edges feel firm and a skewer inserted into the center comes out with moist crumbs attached, 18 to 20 minutes. Let cool completely in the pan.

Run a knife along the inside edge of the pan to release the brownie. Place a large piece of aluminum foil on a flat work surface. Invert the pan over the foil to release the brownie. Trim about ¼ in [6 mm] from the edges, and then cut the brownie in half across the center to make two rectangles, each about 10 by 7 in [25 by 17 cm].

To assemble, soften the ice cream slightly. Spread the ice cream gently and evenly over one of the brownie halves. Place the other brownie half, walnut-side up, on top of the ice cream; gently compress to flatten the sandwich and bring the ice cream out to the edges. Wrap the foil securely around the brownie and freeze until firm, at least 8 hours or up to 2 days.

Remove the brownie from the freezer and remove the foil. Using a sharp knife, cut into 12 rectangles. Serve the sandwiches immediately, or wrap individually in plastic wrap and freeze for up to 2 days.

MAKES 12 SANDWICHES

ICE CREAM BONBONS

2 pt [960 ml] premium ice cream, any flavor

1 lb [455 g] bittersweet chocolate, finely chopped

3 Tbsp nonhydrogenated solid vegetable shortening

Freeze a baking sheet for about 20 minutes.

Soften 1 pt [480 ml] of the ice cream slightly (work with one container of ice cream at a time to avoid melting the second one), just until soft enough to scoop. Remove the baking sheet from the freezer and line it with parchment or wax paper.

Use a small 1-in [2.5-cm] ice-cream scoop to scoop the ice cream into compact balls, and place them on the baking sheet. Repeat with the second container of ice cream (move the baking sheet into the freezer as you work if the ice cream balls begin to melt). Wrap the pan tightly in plastic wrap to prevent ice crystals from forming. Freeze until the ice cream is very hard, at least 8 hours but preferably overnight.

Line a second baking sheet with parchment or wax paper and place it in the freezer to chill while you melt the chocolate. (This sheet will hold the bonbons after they have been dipped in chocolate.)

CONT'D

Bring about 2 in [5 cm] of water to a boil in a saucepan or the bottom of a double boiler; remove from the heat. Combine the chocolate and shortening in a heatproof bowl or in the top of the double boiler. Set the bowl over the hot water and let stand, stirring occasionally with a flexible spatula, until melted and smooth, about 15 minutes. Remove from the heat and let stand until lukewarm but still fluid, 15 to 20 minutes.

Remove both baking sheets from the freezer and unwrap the ice-cream balls. Working quickly, drop one ice-cream ball at a time into the chocolate mixture. Roll it quickly in the chocolate to coat, and then lift it out, cradling the bottom of the bonbon with your fingertips in a loose claw shape. Shake it gently to let excess chocolate drip off, and place it on the second baking sheet. If the undipped ice-cream balls start to melt as they're waiting to be dipped, return the pan to the freezer and remove one ball at a time as you continue to dip them.

Place the sheet of dipped bonbons in the freezer for about 1 hour. Transfer to an airtight container with a piece of wax paper between each layer and freeze for up to 1 week.

MAKES ABOUT 24 BONBONS